Copyright © 2022 ANETTE BRAND

This work is copyright-free to the purchaser: copies may be made without fee or prior permission provided that the work has been paid for and such copies are used solely within the institution for which the work is purchased.

Brand, Anette (Author)
Academic Language Functions: Advanced
ISBN 978-1-922890-10-8
Educational
Language

Typeset RNS Sanz 11/18

Cover and interior photos by Adobe Stock
Cover and book design by Green Hill Publishing

Academic Language Functions
Advanced

ANETTE BRAND

PREFACE

This photocopiable classroom resource will provide the educator with appropriate content to teach **academic language functions** to:
- secondary school students (Yr. 10 - 12)
- adult ESL learners, and
- individuals who need test preparation for academic IELTS

A **scaffolded approach** has been adopted to support students in their learning:

STAGE 1: Students acquire the necessary vocabulary of a particular language function.

STAGE 2: Students engage in a class activity using the language acquired.

STAGE 3: Students play a board game, using the target language to develop their speaking and listening skills.

STAGE 4: Students use the target language in a short writing exercise.

The materials in this book aim to engage students and **promote interactive learning.**

CONTENTS

COMPARE + CONTRAST — 1

    Language in context — 3
    Activity: describe similarities and differences — 4
    Board game — 5
    Writing task: describe a graph — 8
    Answers — 9

CAUSE + EFFECT — 11

    Language in context — 13
    Activity: identify signal words and phrases — 14
    Board game — 15
    Writing task: paragraph writing — 18
    Answers — 19

EXPRESSING OPINIONS — 21

    Language in context — 23
    Activity: identify appropriate language — 24
    Board game — 25
    Writing task: construct well-formulated opinions — 28
    Answers — 29

DISCUSSION – A BALANCED DEBATE　　　　　　　　　　　　　31

    Language in context　　　　　　　　　　　　　　　　　　33
    Activity: gap-fill exercise　　　　　　　　　　　　　　　　34
    Board game　　　　　　　　　　　　　　　　　　　　　　35
    Writing task: paragraph writing　　　　　　　　　　　　　38
    Answers　　　　　　　　　　　　　　　　　　　　　　　39

PROBLEMS AND SOLUTIONS　　　　　　　　　　　　　　41

    Language in context　　　　　　　　　　　　　　　　　　43
    Activity: analyse sentences　　　　　　　　　　　　　　　44
    Board game　　　　　　　　　　　　　　　　　　　　　　46
    Writing task: paragraph writing　　　　　　　　　　　　　50
    Answers　　　　　　　　　　　　　　　　　　　　　　　51

TOPIC ONE

COMPARE + CONTRAST

Compare + Contrast

LANGUAGE IN CONTEXT

- to **compare** is to refer to **similarities**
- to **contrast** is to refer to **differences**

PAPER BAGS
- biodegradable
- can be composted
- not suitable for wet products
- more water and energy used in manufacturing process
- heavier

Overlap (both):
- can be recycled
- wide range of styles
- many different colours
- has environmental impact
- used as shopping bags
- used as packaging

PLASTIC BAGS
- not biodegradable
- danger to marine life
- lightweight
- can be reused many times
- manufacturing is more environmentally friendly

Language to describe similarities

- **Both** paper bags and plastic bags can be recycled.
- **Like** plastic bags, paper bags come in a variety of sizes and styles.
- Paper bags and plastic bags **are similar in that** they can cause a threat to the environment.
- Plastic bags **as well as** paper bags are used in supermarkets and retail stores.
- **Just as** paper bags can be used for packaging goods, so can plastic bags.
- Plastic bags come in many different colours. **Similarly, / In the same way,** paper bags can be very colourful.

Language to describe differences

- Paper bags and plastic bags **differ in** the number of times that each can be reused.
- **Compared with** plastic bags, paper bags are heavier. (Sometimes, we use **compared to.**)
- Paper bags are not suitable for wet or leaking products. **In contrast,** plastic bags can be used for all kinds of items.
- **Unlike** paper bags, plastic bags can be a danger to marine life due to water pollution.
- Plastic bags are not biodegradable. **On the other hand**, paper bags are biodegradable, and some can be composted.
- The manufacturing of plastic bags is **more** environmentally friendly **than** the manufacturing of paper bags.
- The manufacturing of paper bags requires significant resources, **whereas / while / but** less resources are required to produce plastic bags.

ACTIVITY: DESCRIBE SIMILARITIES AND DIFFERENCES

1. Choose one of the following topics:
   - cash vs credit cards
   - tennis vs badminton
   - tigers vs zebras
   - Facebook vs Tik Tok

2. Brainstorm ideas and complete the Venn diagram.

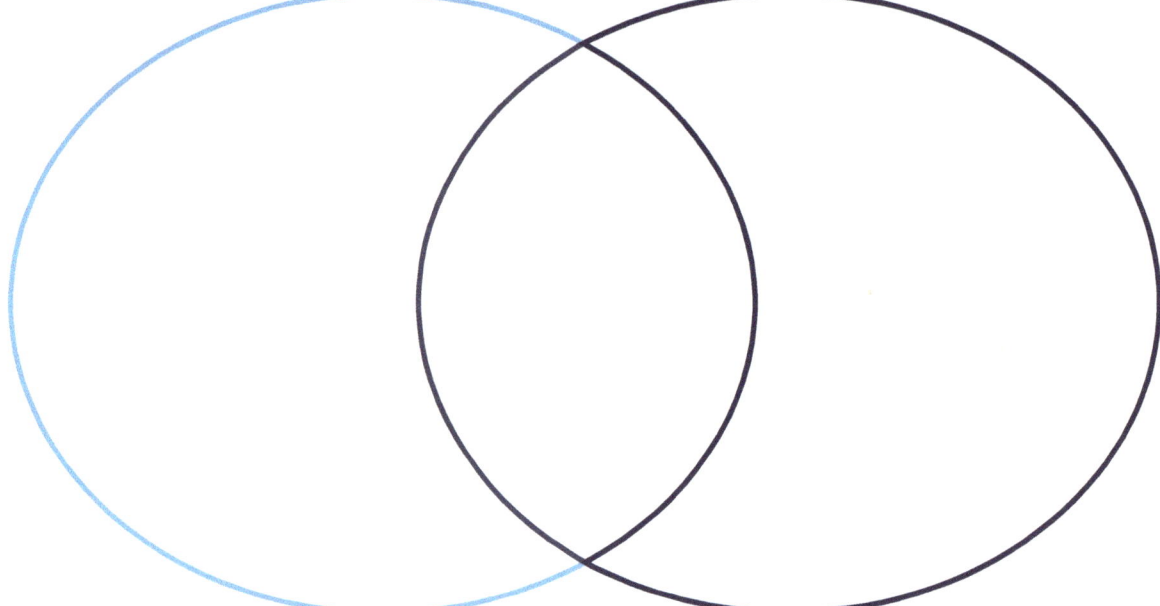

3. Write sentences to describe **similarities**.

   _____
   _____
   _____
   _____

4. Write sentences to describe **differences**.

   _____
   _____
   _____
   _____

BOARD GAME

Board game setup
- photocopy board game as A3
- form groups of 3 to 4 students per group
- give each group the board game, counters and a dice

Board game rules
1. All counters need to be on the 'start' square.
2. To begin, each member of the group rolls the dice. The person with the highest number (1 to 6) will start the game. Rotate clockwise.
3. When a person lands on a square, he/she talks about the **similarities** and **differences** of the topic shown.

> Examples:
> "**Both** KFC and McDonald's are fast food outlets."
> "**Unlike** McDonald's, KFC serves mainly fried chicken."

4. Students are encouraged to use as much of the target language as possible.
5. To avoid repetition, students roll the dice again if they land on the same square as a fellow group member.
6. The winner is the first group member to finish the game.

WRITING TASK: DESCRIBE A GRAPH

Two friends, Jack and Jill, share an apartment. They get along very well even though they have different interests and hobbies. They are also financially responsible and try to keep to their individual budgets.

The graph below shows how they spend their monthly income. Write 2 sentences for each category in the graph, focusing on the **similarities** and **differences**.

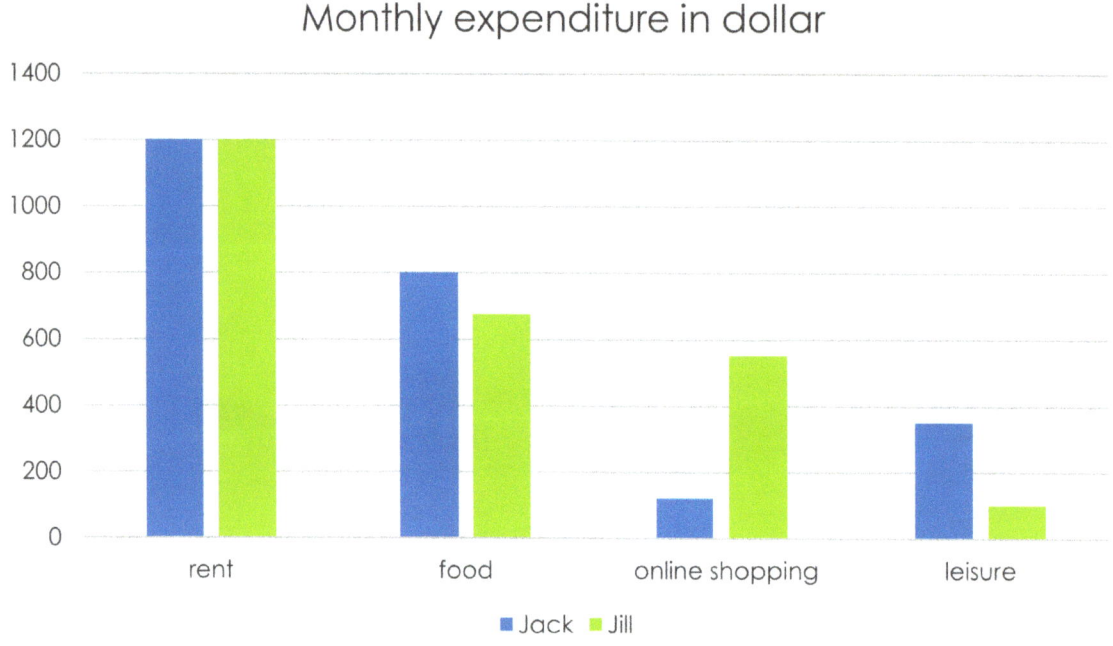

ANSWERS: COMPARE + CONTRAST

p. 4
Follow the examples on p.3

p. 8
Model sentences

Both Jack and Jill spend $1200 on rent per month.

Compared with Jack, Jill splurges nearly $400 more on online purchases.

Jill pays around $700 for food, whereas Jack pays $800 for food every month.

Jill spends about $100 per month on leisure activities. In contrast, Jack spends approximately three times more.

Note
The difference between the use of **'compared with'** and **'compared to'** should be explained.

TOPIC TWO
CAUSE + EFFECT

Cause + Effect

LANGUAGE IN CONTEXT

Cause and **Effect** refer to the relationship between
- events (e.g. natural disasters)
- behaviours (e.g. cyber bullying)
- conditions (e.g. stress)

Topic: Obesity in children

Why do children become obese?   **What** happens when children become obese?

CAUSES	EFFECTS
genetics/overweight parents	can grow into obese adults
overconsumption of foods high in fat or sugar	health problems such as asthma and diabetes
lack of physical activity	body image problems/social isolation

Signal words/phrases for cause and effect relationships:

CAUSE	EFFECT
• for	• so
• because of	• thus/therefore
• since	• consequently
• as (it/they)	• as a result
• due to	• bring/brought about
• owing to	• result/resulted in
• one (possible) cause is	• hence
• can be caused by	• for this reason
• another reason is	• has/have/can have/had an effect
• result/resulted from	• can lead to/contribute to/interfere with
• is/was the result of	• can give rise to/can cause

Example:

                                       CAUSE

Many people struggle to maintain a healthy weight **because of** their genetic makeup.

                                       EFFECT

The overconsumption of junk food is prevalent amongst younger people. **As a result**, many children and adolescents are being diagnosed with serious health problems.

ACTIVITY: IDENTIFY SIGNAL WORDS AND PHRASES

Task
- underline the cause and effect signal words/phrases in the following sentences
- put a 'C' for cause and an 'E' for effect

                                                                  C

1. A reluctance to take part in physical activities could be <u>one possible cause</u> for the increase in the number of obese children.

2. Owing to a global increase in the demand for electric vehicles, the price of EV batteries has dropped significantly.

3. There are real fears that several bee species are on the brink of extinction. Therefore, there is a strong push for more ecological farming practices.

4. Studies have shown that excessive exposure to noise can have a detrimental effect on a person's cardiovascular system.

5. Netflix is the most popular streaming service as it is good value for money.

6. The availability of party drugs at music festivals has become a serious concern; consequently, authorities have taken several steps to combat this issue.

7. Phobias and fears should be taken seriously, for conditions such as arachnophobia can interfere with an individual's normal life.

8. Watching 'Funny Cat' videos on YouTube is a popular pastime since they provide endless entertainment.

BOARD GAME

Board game setup
- photocopy board game as A3
- form groups of 3 to 4 students per group
- give each group the board game, counters and a dice

Board game rules
1. All counters need to be on the 'start' square.
2. To begin, each member of the group rolls the dice. The person with the highest number (1 to 6) will start the game. Rotate clockwise.
3. When a person lands on a square, he/she talks about the **causes** or **effects** of the topic shown.

> **Examples:**
> "Many parents home-school their children **due to** the prevalence of bullying in traditional school settings."
>
> "Being an only child **can lead to** antisocial behaviour."

4. Students are encouraged to use as much of the target language as possible.
5. To avoid repetition, students roll the dice again if they land on the same square as a fellow group member.
6. The winner is the first group member to finish the game.

CAUSE + EFFECT

Start

- reasons for home-schooling
- effects of being an only child
- road rage causes
- impact of divorce on families
- impacts of malnutrition on young children
- reasons for banning phones in school
- reasons for video game addiction
- causes of debt
- effects of diabetes
- effects of animal testing

Finish

- reasons for stress
- reasons for cosmetic surgery
- miss a turn
- effects of long-distance dating
- effects of regular exercise

KEY WORDS AND PHRASES

because of	therefore
due to	as a result
since	can give rise to
as	for this reason
one possible cause is	can lead to
for	had an effect
resulted from	hence
can be caused by	so
another reason is	resulted in

WRITING TASK: PARAGRAPH WRITING

Read the text about household waste and complete the final paragraph by using the target language.

Household waste – a losing battle

Many countries around the world have taken up the battle against household waste. Authorities are constantly discussing new strategies, while several recycling programs to curb the growing waste problem have been launched with various degrees of success. It seems that finding a solution to address this issue could be quite the challenge in the world we live in today.

One of the main reasons why household waste has increased exponentially is packaging. In most supermarkets, customers can buy packaged fruit and vegetables, **therefore** eliminating the need for the consumer to pick up fresh produce and put it in a bag. Such convenience **could** very well **result in** more products being wrapped up in plastic and polystyrene, to cater to a new breed of shopper. Also, **due to** the rise of food delivery companies such as UberEats and Menulog, more and more people prefer to order in. **Consequently,** rubbish bins are now overflowing with plastic containers and other packaging materials. Although people are encouraged to put plastic containers in the recycling bin, many do not **because** they cannot be bothered to rinse out the containers.

Another reason why we are drowning in household waste is the rise of consumerism. It seems that we cannot get enough of shopping online. **As a result,** packages of all shapes and sizes arrive on our doorstep on a regular basis and it soon becomes a real bubble wrap fest! There is also a distinct shift in consumer culture. Gone are the days when people held on to whitegoods, technology or even furniture for a long time. **Since** we have adopted the attitude of *out with the old and in with the new*, landfill is clogged up with unwanted items. **Thus**, it seems that we are losing the war on waste.

A lack of leadership from authorities also **contributes to** the problem of waste management.

_____
_____
_____
_____
_____
_____
_____
_____
_____

ANSWERS: CAUSE + EFFECT

p. 14

    C
2. **Owing to** a global increase in the demand for electric vehicles, the price of EV batteries has dropped significantly.

                                                                                                              E
3. There are real fears that several bee species are on the brink of extinction. **Therefore,** there is a strong push for more ecological farming practices.

                                                       E
4. Studies have shown that excessive exposure to noise **can have** a detrimental effect on a person's cardiovascular system.

                                          C
5. Netflix is the most popular streaming service **as** it is good value for money.

                                                                                                                        E
6. The availability of party drugs at music festivals has become a serious concern; **consequently,** authorities have taken several steps to combat this issue.

7. Phobias and fears should be taken seriously, for conditions such as arachnophobia can **interfere with** an individual's normal life.

          E   C
8. Watching 'Funny Cat' videos on YouTube is a popular pastime **since** they provide endless entertainment.

p. 18

Model answer

A lack of leadership from authorities also **contributes to** the problem of waste management. Local councils have been slow to come up with initiatives to change people's waste disposal habits. **Hence,** every week overflowing rubbish bins are being put out to be collected by waste disposal companies. Some councils have provided households with small compost caddies to reduce food waste. However, limited success has been achieved **owing to** a lack of information and education provided to residents. The inaction from local government organisations **can contribute to** environmental problems which may threaten the sustainability of the Earth.

TOPIC THREE
EXPRESSING OPINIONS

Expressing Opinions

LANGUAGE IN CONTEXT

Animals should live in their natural habitat and not be kept in zoos.

To what extent do you agree or disagree? Tick one of the following boxes:

- ☐ I agree 100% with the statement
- ☐ I disagree 100% with the statement
- ☐ I agree/disagree partially with the statement

Outline of a response	LANGUAGE	
1. Express opinion	**Personal point of view** • **verbs** I *think* that … I *believe* that … I *feel* that … I *can see* that … I *suppose* … I *guess* … • **adverbial phrases** In my opinion, / In my view, … In my experience, … As far as I'm concerned, … • **adverbs** Actually, … Quite frankly, … Personally, …	**General point of view** • **verbs** Some people *say/think* that … Many *feel/believe* that … Everybody *knows* that … It *is thought* that … It *is* a well-known fact that … Studies *seem* to suggest that … • **adverbial phrases** In general. … According to … • **adverbs** Apparently, …
2. Give reason(s)	because … / since … / because of … / due to … / as …	
3. Give example(s)	For example, / For instance, … To give you an example, / Let me give you an example, … Let me illustrate, / To elaborate, … Firstly, / Secondly, / Also, etc. …	
4. Restate opinion	Therefore, I … So, I …	

Example:

Personally, I feel that zoos play an important role in wildlife conservation **as** they provide a safe environment for endangered animals. **For instance,** current data suggests that nearly 60% of primates are at risk of becoming extinct. **Therefore,** it is my opinion that animals should be kept in zoos to ensure their survival.

ACTIVITY: IDENTIFY APPROPRIATE LANGUAGE

Task

Underline the correct word/phrase in the sentences below.

1. **Personally, / Surprisingly,** I think that advertising that promotes gambling should be banned from all sporting events.
2. **Actually, / According to** my lecturer there will be two assessments at the end of the term.
3. Many people **guess / believe** that climate change is a pressing issue **because of / as** an increase in severe weather events.
4. In my opinion, more should be done to encourage new mothers to re-join the workforce after maternity leave. **For example, / Apparently**, providing access to affordable and reliable childcare must be a priority for all employers.
5. **Everybody knows that / Personally**, smoking can cause serious health issues such as heart disease.
6. As far as I'm concerned, corporal punishment does not have a place in modern society **due to / because** the detrimental effects it has on children.
7. **I strongly believe / Therefore, I believe** that live animal exports should be banned because it is a cruel practice. **Firstly, / So,** too many animals are loaded onto vessels which result in suffocation and death. **Since / Also,** in some countries inhumane slaughtering methods are used with many of the livestock suffering a slow and painful death.
8. **Many vegans feel strongly that / In general**, the environment will be better off if people stop eating meat. **I suppose / It is a well-known fact** that this may be true but banning all meat products could cripple a country's economy.
9. A suggestion by the authorities to fine people $1000 for using their mobile phone while driving has caused an outcry. **I suppose / Quite frankly**, I'm all for it **as / because of** too many accidents happen **as / because of** mobile phone distraction.
10. **For instance, / In my experience**, working from home is a good option **also / as** it can increase productivity. **To elaborate, / Therefore,** instead of facing hours trapped in traffic jams people can use their time more effectively. **Also, / So,** when employees are feeling unwell, they do not have to take sick days **because / due to** they are already at home. **For example, / So**, working from home sounds like an excellent idea to me!

BOARD GAME

Board game setup
- photocopy board game as A3
- form groups of 3 to 4 students per group
- give each group the board game, counters and a dice

Board game rules
1. All counters need to be on the 'start' square.
2. To begin, each member of the group rolls the dice. The person with the highest number (1 to 6) will start the game. Rotate clockwise.
3. When a person lands on a square, he/she **gives** his/her **opinion** on the topic shown.

> **Example:**
> "**I think** that bottled water should not be banned **because** it can save the lives of people. **For example**, during a flood the water supply of a town can become contaminated and undrinkable. **So, I believe** that bottled water is a useful commodity."

4. Students are encouraged to use as much of the target language as possible.
5. To avoid repetition, students roll the dice again if they land on the same square as a fellow group member.
6. The winner is the first group member to finish the game.

WHAT IS YOUR OPINION?

Start

- Public transport is too expensive.
- Success is determined by hard work only.
- Recreational drugs should be legalised.
- Delivery drones are the future.
- Capital punishment will reduce crime rates.
- Renewable energy should replace all fossil fuels.
- Organ donation should be encouraged.
- Stricter gun control is needed.
- Bottled water should be banned.
- Money can buy happiness.

Finish

- PERSONALLY
- Primary school students should not get any homework.
- Spell the word:
- FOMO can affect a person's mental health.
- A sugar tax will help to reduce obesity.

KEY WORDS AND PHRASES

First of all,
Actually,
I believe that
because of
Many feel that

Frankly,
In general,
According to
Apparently,

Board game spaces (following the path):

- Diets are a waste of time.
- Marriage should be for life.
- GM foods can solve world hunger.
- Extra turn
- Online privacy does not exist.
- Climate change is real.
- Young people are self-centred.
- Capitalism benefits only the rich.
- Globalisation destroys culture.
- Space exploration is not worth the cost.
- There are too many charities.
- Move 2 spaces forward
- Reality TV shows are good entertainment.
- Party balloons cause pollution.
- Move 3 spaces forward
- Gender equality is not possible.
- Students receive a better education in a private school.
- Everyone should learn a new language.
- Vitamin supplements are a waste of money.
- Some extreme sports are too extreme.
- Back to start

WRITING TASK: CONSTRUCT WELL-FORMULATED OPINIONS

Write down your opinion about the following statements.
Follow the 4 steps in the outline.

1. The ancient practice of meditation should be taught in schools.

2. Prison is not always the best punishment for people who have committed a crime.

3. Millennials are the loneliest generation.

4. Food expiration dates are meaningless and should be ignored.

5. Arranged marriages have a better chance of succeeding.

ANSWERS: EXPRESSING OPINIONS

p. 24

1. Personally,
2. According to
3. believe; because of
4. For example,
5. Everybody knows that
6. due to
7. I strongly believe; Firstly; Also,
8. Many vegans feel strongly that; I suppose
9. Quite frankly; as; because of
10. In my experience; as; To elaborate; Also; because; So

p. 28
Student answers

TOPIC FOUR
DISCUSSION – A BALANCED DEBATE

DISCUSSION – a balanced debate

LANGUAGE IN CONTEXT

To look at an issue objectively, we need to have a balanced discussion. Therefore, we **discuss/investigate/examine/explain** the

- advantages and disadvantages
- benefits and drawbacks
- pros and cons
- positive and negative results
- beneficial and detrimental impacts

of the issue.

The Language

Acknowledging that there are two sides to the issue in the introduction
- There are two sides to …
- This issue has positive and negative impacts on …
- Although there are many advantages …, there are also significant disadvantages.

Introducing arguments
- One major advantage / beneficial result is …
- Supporters of … claim that …
- First of all, / Firstly, …
- Another aspect is …
- Moreover, / In addition, / Also, / Furthermore, / Additionally, …

Introducing an opposing point of view
- Opponents / Critics of … claim / argue / believe that …
- On the other hand, …
- In contrast, / On the contrary, …
- However, …

Giving examples
- For example, / For instance, / An example of this is …
- …, especially / …, particularly / …, mainly
- …, such as …
- Use words that indicate modality: perhaps / possibly / maybe / often / probably / apparently / It appears to be …

Concluding with a viewpoint
- It is evident that …
- So, all in all I believe that …
- While it may be true that … has many benefits, we cannot ignore the drawbacks.
- When it comes to …, the pros outweigh the cons.

ACTIVITY: GAP-FILL EXERCISE

During a pandemic it should be compulsory to wear a face mask in public. Discuss.

Choose the correct word(s) from the box to fill in the blanks.

probably	On the other hand	In addition
advantages	may	believe
disadvantages	Furthermore	For example

The world is facing a new threat – the spread of highly transmissible diseases such as the coronavirus. Governments and health authorities are faced with the task to develop and implement measures that will curb the spread to keep people from becoming infected. One such measure is to make the wearing of face masks compulsory in public settings. Although the advantages of wearing a face mask during a pandemic have been well documented, there are (1)_____ too.

One of the main (2)_____ of face masks is that they slow down the transmission of viruses. When infected people cough, sneeze, or even sing, they release droplets in the air. These airborne droplets can be inhaled by others who then can become infected. (3)_____, people get influenza or the common cold by being near others who are infected with the virus and who do not wear any face covering. (4)_____, wearing a face mask can protect people from contracting diseases such as the coronavirus which is highly contagious. Face masks are (5)_____ the best line of defence during a pandemic.

(6)_____, making face masks compulsory could cause more harm than good. One drawback of face masks is that they can make people feel claustrophobic. Having their noses and mouths covered could make them feel that they do not get enough oxygen. This (7)_____ cause anxiety or even breathing problems, especially for those who suffer from asthma. (8)_____, certain groups believe that it is an abuse of fundamental human rights to force people to wear face masks. They are opposed to the idea that governments limit the personal freedom of individuals.

In conclusion, face masks are highly effective in the fight against highly contagious diseases. Although exceptions could be made for medical reasons, I (9)_____ that it should be compulsory to wear face masks in public during a pandemic.

BOARD GAME

Board game setup
- photocopy board game as A3
- form groups of 3 to 4 students per group
- give each group the board game, counters and a dice

Board game rules
1. All counters need to be on the 'start' square.
2. To begin, each member of the group rolls the dice. The person with the highest number (1 to 6) will start the game. Rotate clockwise.
3. When a person lands on a square, he/she talks about the **advantages** or **disadvantages** of the topic shown.

> **Example:**
> **"One major advantage** of taking part in sport is the health benefits. When people are physically active their heart rate goes up, which helps their bodies to burn more calories. This is **particularly** beneficial for those individuals who have health issues such as high cholesterol."

4. Students are encouraged to use as much of the target language as possible.
5. To avoid repetition, students roll the dice again if they land on the same square as a fellow group member.
6. The winner is the first group member to finish the game.

WRITING TASK: PARAGRAPH WRITING

Discuss the benefits and drawbacks of studying online.

1. Brainstorm benefits and drawbacks

   +   -

   +   -

   +   -

2. Write a paragraph about the benefits of studying online.

_____
_____
_____
_____
_____
_____
_____
_____
_____
_____

3. Write a paragraph about the drawbacks of studying online.

_____
_____
_____
_____
_____
_____
_____
_____
_____
_____

ANSWERS: DISCUSSION

p. 34

1. disadvantages
2. advantages
3. For example
4. In addition/Furthermore
5. probably
6. On the other hand
7. may
8. Furthermore/In addition
9. believe

p. 38

Students refer to the example essay on p.34.
'During a pandemic it should be compulsory to wear a face mask in public. Discuss.'

TOPIC FIVE
PROBLEMS AND SOLUTIONS

PROBLEMS AND SOLUTIONS

LANGUAGE IN CONTEXT

Global Issues

Brainstorm

Social problems: _____

Environmental problems: _____

Health problems: _____

Economic problems: _____

Once the causes and effects of a problem are identified, solutions can be found.

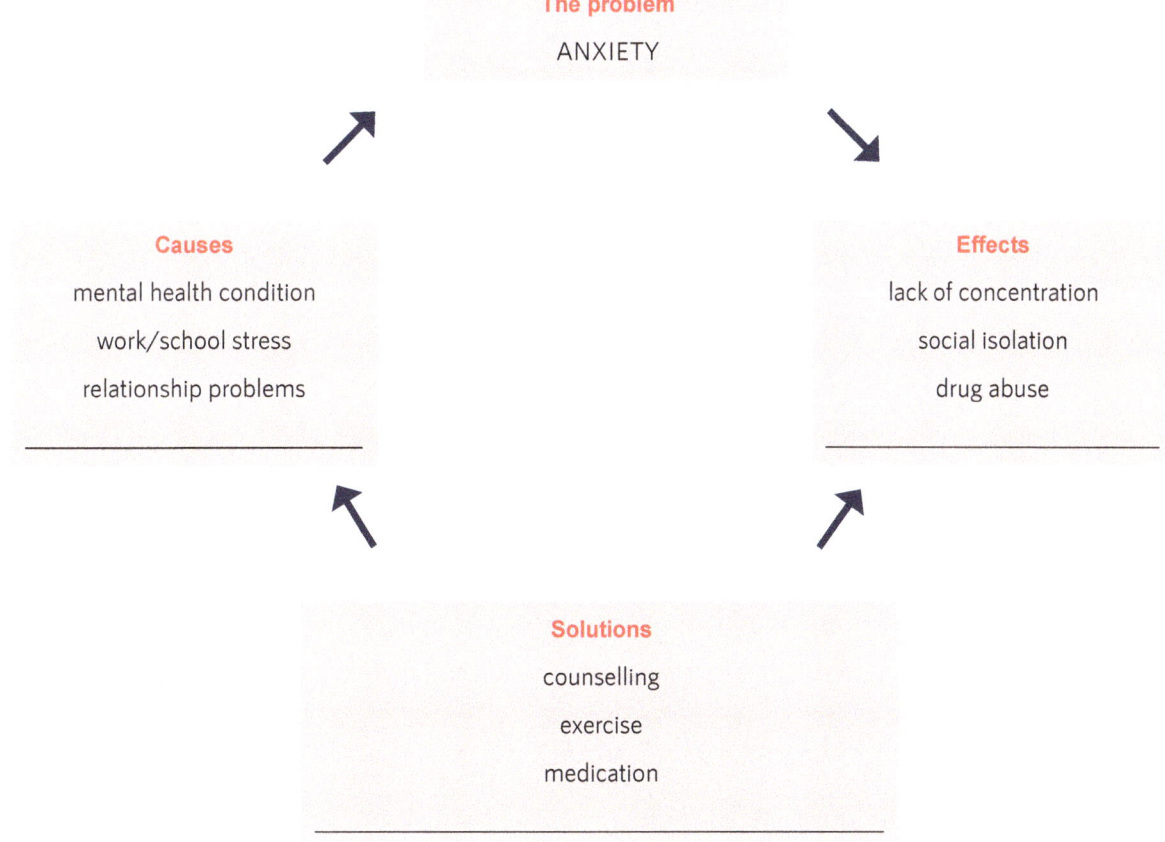

The problem
ANXIETY

Causes
mental health condition
work/school stress
relationship problems
_____

Effects
lack of concentration
social isolation
drug abuse
_____

Solutions
counselling
exercise
medication
_____

The Language

The problem	Provide a solution	Justify response
Animal cruelty	One way to address this issue is to report incidents of animal cruelty to the authorities.	If this is done, the offenders can be punished.
Climate change	A good solution to this problem is for industries to reduce their greenhouse gas emissions.	As a result, climate change will be slowed down.
Child screen addiction	One step that can be taken to solve this problem is to encourage children to play sports.	This would provide an alternative form of entertainment for young people.
World hunger	Actions to reduce world hunger could include sustainable farming practices.	Due to improved soil conditions, healthier food will be produced which could alleviate world hunger.
Opposition to vaccines	Educating vaccination sceptics could be a step in the right direction.	Unless action is taken, the health of the wider population might be at risk.

ACTIVITY: ANALYSE SENTENCES

Read the following sentences and
1. identify the problem with a **(P)**
2. identify the solution given (what to do) with an **(S)**
3. <u>underline</u> the supporting sentences (how to do it / why it is a good idea)
4. identify the justification with a **(J)**

Example:
                                   P   **S**

One way to address the issue of **(online abuse)** is to **(block and delete the person responsible from all contact lists)**. <u>A quick Google search will assist in the processes needed to successfully safeguard an individual from online trolls. The Internet provides clear instructions for several devices, including iPhones and android phones. For example, the phone user will be prompted to access their contact list, select the person to be blocked or deleted, before tapping Block.</u> **(If this is done, the victim will be protected from future attacks).**
              J

1. Steps that can be taken to reduce e-waste include the development of biodegradable electronic gadgets. Biodegradable plastic products are already widely used in developed countries, including shopping bags and take-away containers. Plans to make components of e-waste biodegradable too have gained traction in countries such as Germany. Currently, there is a lack of funding for such endeavours; however, with support from governments, this initiative can significantly reduce e-waste. By making electronics more eco-friendly, a more sustainable planet can be achieved.

2. One step that can be taken to deal with loneliness is to become a volunteer. Volunteering provides many opportunities to play an active role in the community. For example, aged-care facilities are in desperate need of volunteers to provide companionship and care to their residents. By interacting with the elderly, volunteers can create positive experiences for the aged-care residents and their families. Also, staff and volunteers work together to improve services. As a result, people who work as volunteers will feel more connected to others and less lonely.

3. Actions to combat a sedentary lifestyle could include active hobbies such as salsa dancing. Dancing is an enjoyable activity that brings smiles and spreads laughter. The upbeat tempo of salsa music brings a fun element to salsa dancing, while dancers also get lots of exercise. As a result, endorphins are released, which enhances feelings of positivity and happiness. Salsa dancing is also a social activity where dancers can partner up with other dancers. Not only will such a fun activity be good for the individual's physical health, but it will also provide opportunities to form new friendships.

4. A good solution to prevent road rage is for motorists to accept that all humans can make mistakes. In an ideal world, we would prefer that drivers always pay attention to the road. However, people are not robots and, therefore, not always emotionally stable. For instance, when people receive distressing news, it could impact their driving ability. Also, elderly drivers might not react as quickly, as their reflexes slow with age. If road users are more considerate and tolerant towards other drivers, it will make our roads a safer place.

BOARD GAME

Board game setup
- photocopy board game as A3
- form groups of 3 to 4 students per group
- give each group the board game, counters and a dice

Board game rules
1. All counters need to be on the 'start' square.
2. To begin, each member of the group rolls the dice. The person with the highest number (1 to 6) will start the game. Rotate clockwise.
3. When a person lands on a square, he/she discusses the **causes and effects** of the problem and provides a **solution** for the **problem,** and a **justification**.

> **Example: Busy lifestyles**
> "Many struggle to cope with their busy lifestyle **because of** the pressures of work and family. **Consequently**, people are feeling burnt out and stressed. **One step that can be taken** is to delegate tasks if possible, such as sharing the household duties with your spouse. **This would** free up some time to spend on more enjoyable activities."

4. Students are encouraged to use as much of the target language as possible.
5. To avoid repetition, students roll the dice again if they land on the same square as a fellow group member.
6. The winner is the first group member to finish the game.

WRITING TASK: PARAGRAPH WRITING

1. **Choose one of the following topics:**
   - fast fashion
   - overprotective parents

2. **Brainstorm the causes and effects of, and possible solutions for, your chosen problem.**

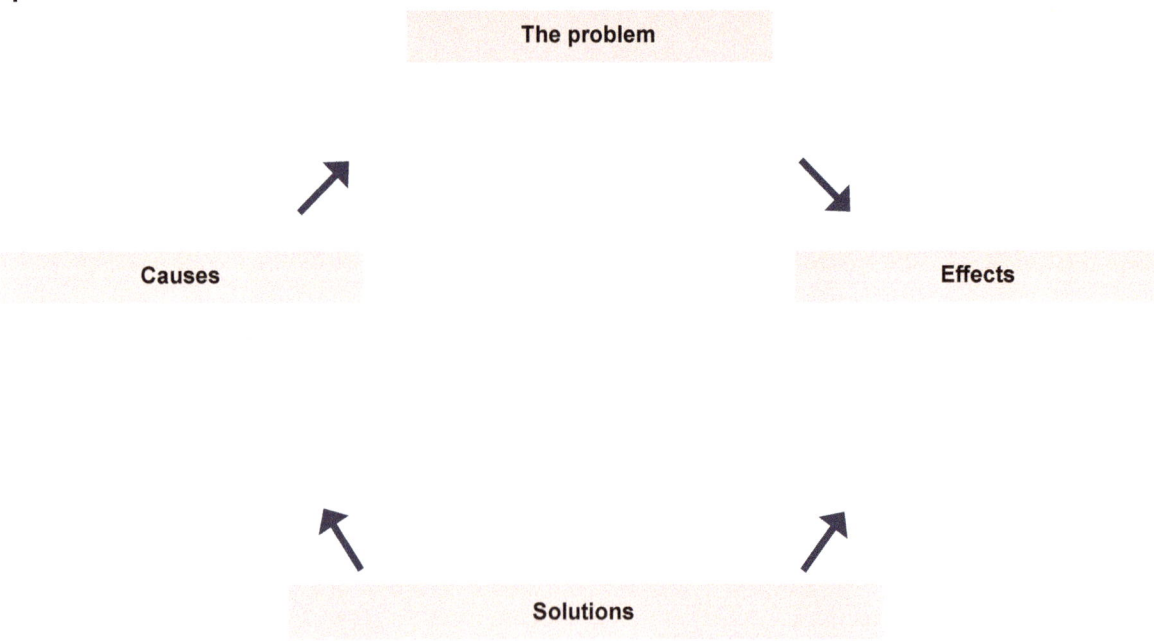

3. **Choose one solution and write a paragraph about it (80 - 100 words). Remember to include a justification. Refer to the examples on pp. 44-45.**

_____
_____
_____
_____
_____
_____
_____
_____
_____

ANSWERS: PROBLEMS and SOLUTIONS

p. 43
Social problems: homelessness, overpopulation, crime, ageism, refugees, etc.
Environmental problems: climate change, pesticides, toxic waste, fossil fuels, etc.
Health problems: substance abuse, mental health issues, skin cancer, etc.
Economic problems: high fuel prices, minimum wage, student loans, etc.

p. 45

1. Steps that can be taken to reduce **P (e-waste)** include **S (the development of biodegradable electronic gadgets)**. Biodegradable plastic products are already widely used in developed countries, including shopping bags and take-away containers. Plans to make components of e-waste biodegradable too have gained traction in countries such as Germany. Currently, there is a lack of funding for such endeavours; however, with support from governments, this initiative can significantly reduce e-waste. **J (By making electronics more eco-friendly, a more sustainable planet can be achieved)**.

2. One step that can be taken to deal with **P (loneliness)** is to **S (become a volunteer)**. Volunteering provides many opportunities to play an active role in the community. For example, aged-care facilities are in desperate need of volunteers to provide companionship and care to their residents. By interacting with the elderly, volunteers can create positive experiences for the aged-care residents and their families. Also, staff and volunteers work together to improve services. **J (As a result, people who work as volunteers will feel more connected to others and less lonely)**.

3. Actions to combat a **P (sedentary lifestyle)** could include active hobbies such as **S (salsa dancing)**. Dancing is an enjoyable activity that brings smiles and spreads laughter. The upbeat tempo of salsa music brings a fun element to salsa dancing, while dancers also get lots of exercise. As a result, endorphins are released, which enhances feelings of positivity and happiness. Salsa dancing is also a social activity where dancers can partner up with other dancers. **J (Not only will such a fun activity be good for the individual's physical health, but it will also provide opportunities to form new friendships)**.

4. A good solution to prevent **P (road rage)** is for motorists to **S (accept that all humans can make mistakes)**. In an ideal world, we would prefer that drivers always pay attention to the road. However, people are not robots and, therefore, not always emotionally stable. For instance, when people receive distressing news, it could impact their driving ability. Also, elderly drivers might not react as quickly, as their reflexes slow with age. **J (If road users are more considerate and tolerant towards other drivers, it will make our roads a safer place).**

p. 50
Refer to the examples on pp. 44 - 45.